CONTENTS

What Do You Wear?

What hat do you wear on your head? What shoes do you wear on your feet?

Children around the world wear all kinds of clothing. Let's see what they wear!

These children live
in the United States.

Dressing for the Weather

Some people live in cold places. They bundle up to keep warm.

A **parka** is a heavy jacket with a furry hood. It keeps you very warm.

parka

These children wear parkas in Canada.

Some people live in hot places. They don't need furry hoods! They need to stay cool.

Wearing a **lavalava** helps this child stay cool. It is a piece of cloth you wrap around your body.

lavalava

This girl wears a lavalava in the Cook Islands.

Clothing can also keep us safe from the sun.

A **turban** is like a long scarf wrapped around your head. It keeps the sun off your head in the desert. You can cover your face with part of the scarf if the sand blows.

turban

This boy wears a turban in Morocco.

At School and Play

What do you wear to school? Many children around the world wear a **uniform**. A uniform can be a dress or a jacket. It can have a tie or a hat.

uniform

These girls wear school uniforms in Cuba.

You may put on **jeans** when it is time to play.

But jeans are not the only clothes for playing. Children run and jump in all kinds of clothes.

jeans

These girls wear play clothes in Peru.

Time to Dress Up!

On special days, children everywhere dress up!

Here, girls may wear **kimonos** for a holiday. A kimono is a long, silk robe. People in this country have worn kimonos for hundreds of years.

These girls wear kimonos in Japan.

kimonos

In some places, dressing up may mean wearing a **kilt**. A kilt is a plaid skirt. In other places, people may put on beautiful **feathers**.

What do *you* wear on a special day?

feathers

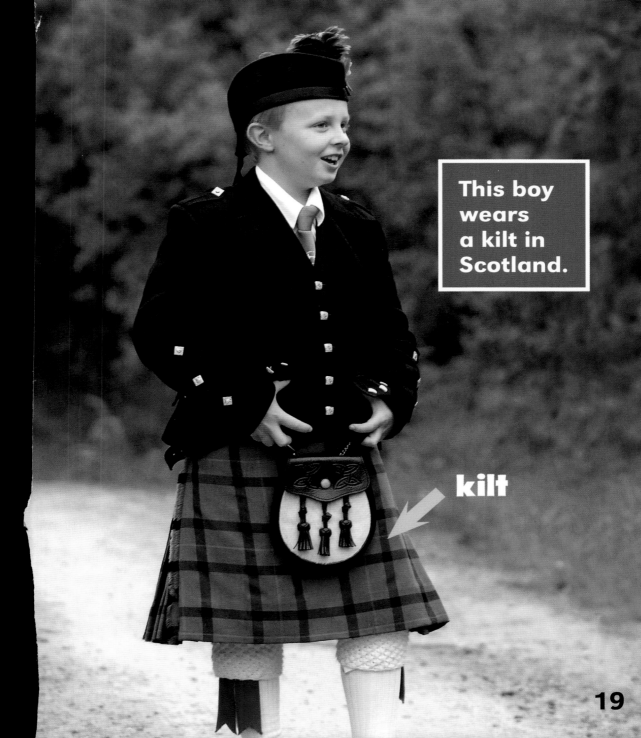

This boy wears a kilt in Scotland.

kilt

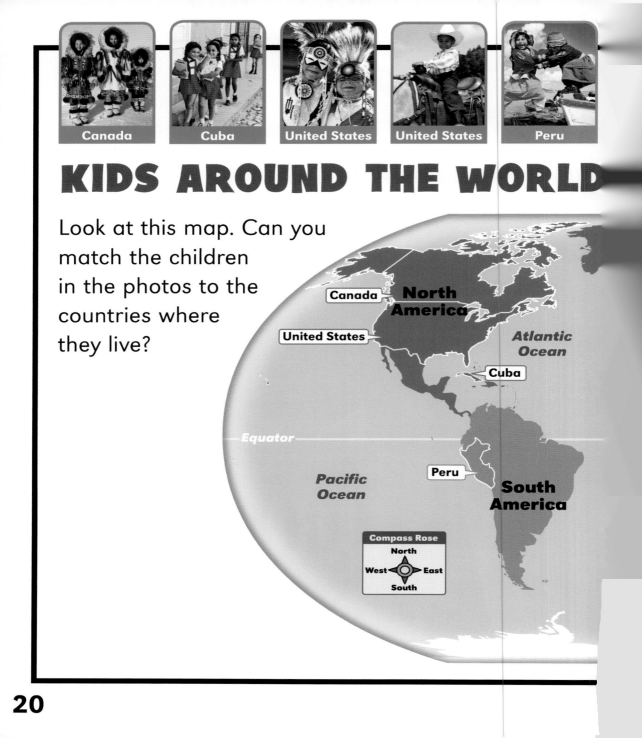

Canada | Cuba | United States | United States | Peru

KIDS AROUND THE WORLD

Look at this map. Can you match the children in the photos to the countries where they live?

Canada

North America

United States

Atlantic Ocean

Cuba

Equator

Pacific Ocean

Peru

South America

Compass Rose
North
West — East
South

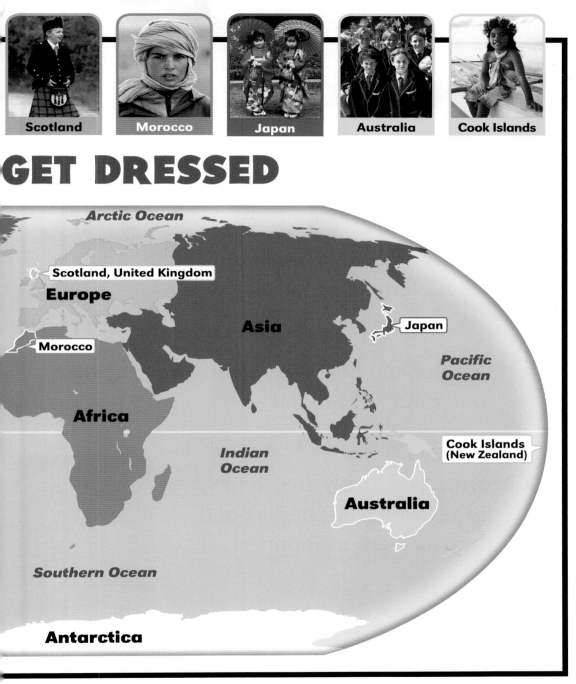

Scotland

Morocco

Japan

Australia

Cook Islands

GET DRESSED

Arctic Ocean

Scotland, United Kingdom

Europe

Asia

Japan

Morocco

Pacific Ocean

Africa

Indian Ocean

Cook Islands (New Zealand)

Australia

Southern Ocean

Antarctica

YOUR NEW WORDS

feathers (**feth**-urz) the light, fluffy pieces covering a bird's body

jeans (jeenz) pants made of strong cloth, used for play or work

kilt (kilt) a plaid skirt with pleats, worn by men and boys in Scotland

kimonos (kuh-**moh**-noz) long robes with wide sleeves and a sash, worn in Japan

lavalava (**lah**-vuh-**lah**-vuh) a piece of printed cloth tied around the body, worn by people in the Pacific islands

parka (**par**-kuh) a heavy, hooded jacket sometimes made with fur

turban (**tur**-buhn) a head covering made by winding a long scarf around the head

uniform (**yoo**-nuh-form) a special set of clothes worn by all the people in a group, like students at a school or police officers

INDEX

FIND OUT MORE
Book:
Morris, Ann. *Hats, Hats, Hats*. New York: HarperCollins, 1993.

Website:
Smithsonian Education
http://africa.si.edu/exhibits/styles/fun4.html

MEET THE AUTHOR
Janice Behrens is a writer and Scholastic editor. She lives with her family in New York City and mostly wears jeans.